THE STORY BEHIND THE SYMBOL

# LIBERTY BELL

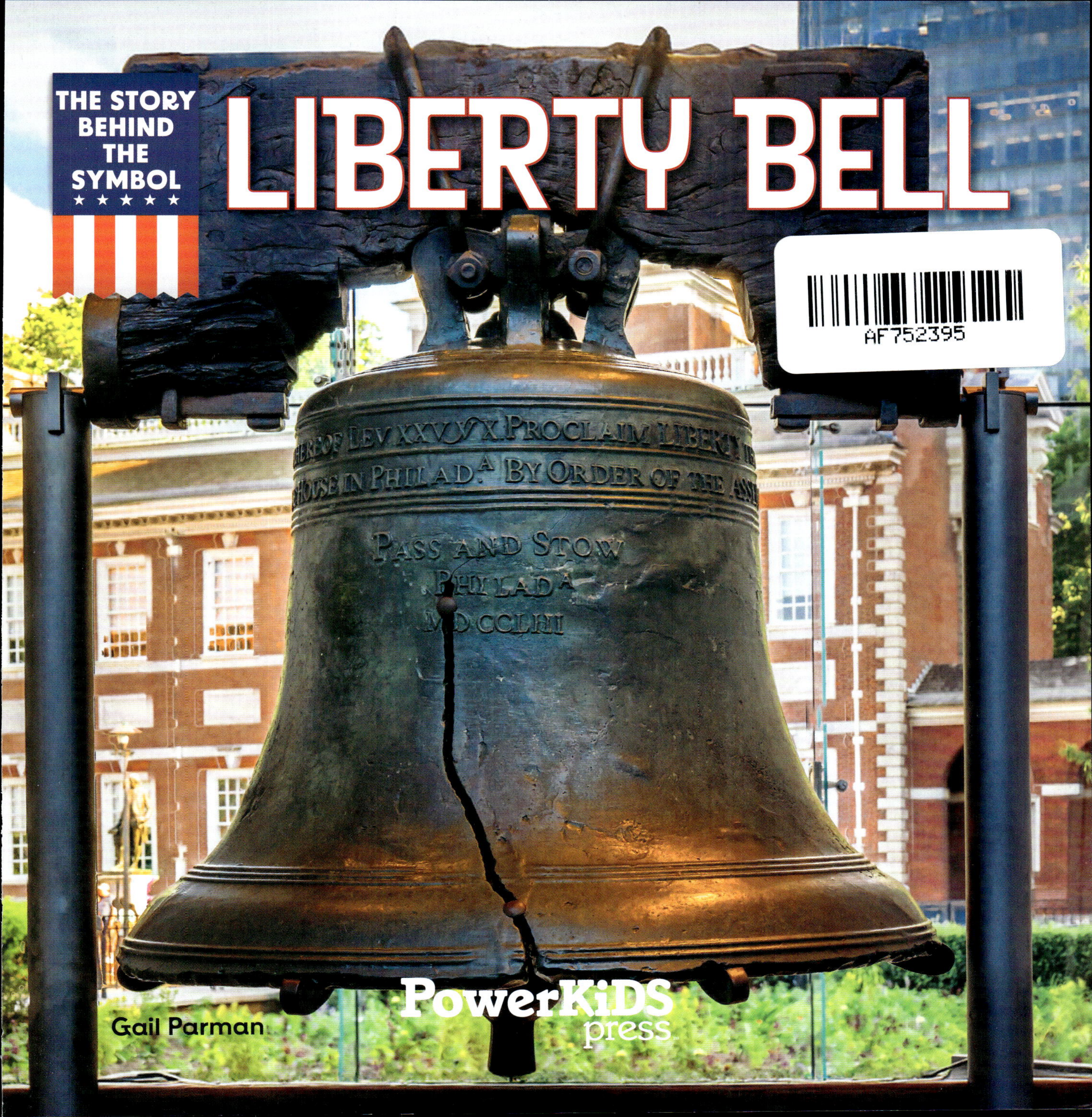




Gail Parman

PowerKiDS press

Published in 2027 by The Rosen Publishing Group, Inc.
2544 Clinton Street, Buffalo, NY 14224



Portions of this work were originally authored by Therese M. Shea and published as *Zoom in on American Symbols: Zoom in on the Liberty Bell.* All new material in this edition is authored by Gail Parman.

Editor: Tricia Hoffman
Book Design: Beeline Media and Design

Photo Credits: Cover, p. 1 foto-select/Shutterstock.com; cover, p. 1, 5, 7, 9, 11, 13, 15, 17, 19, 21 Realstockvector/Shutterstock.com; p. 4 Nancie Lee/Shutterstock.com; p. 5 f11photo/Shutterstock.com; p. 6 Morphart Creation/Morphart Creation; p. 7, 8, 9, 13, 14, 15, 17 Library of Congress/Library of Congress; p. 11 Wikipedia/Shutterstock.com; p. 19 NPS/NPS; p. 20 Marc Cappelletti/Marc Cappelletti; p. 21 f11photo/Shutterstock.com

Cataloging-in-Publication Data
Names: Parman, Gail.
Title: Liberty Bell / Gail Parman.
Description: Buffalo, New York : PowerKids Press, 2027. | Series: The story behind the symbol | Includes glossary and index.
Identifiers: ISBN 9781499458077 (pbk.) | ISBN 9781499458084 (library bound) | ISBN 9781499458091 (ebook)
Subjects: LCSH: Liberty Bell--Juvenile literature. | Signs and symbols--United States--Juvenile literature. | Philadelphia (Pa.)--Buildings, structures, etc.--Juvenile literature.
Classification: LCC F158.8.I3 P377 2027 | DDC 974.811--dc23

Printed in China

CPSIA Compliance Information: Batch #QSPK27. For Further Information contact Rosen Publishing at 1-800-237-9932.

# CONTENTS

# A Special Bell

The Liberty Bell in Philadelphia, Pennsylvania, is a famous American **symbol**. It is well known for the wide crack along its side, but it represents so much more than that. The Liberty Bell represents freedom.

It first came to represent the idea of liberty, or freedom, because of the special words on it: "**Proclaim** Liberty throughout all the Land unto all the **Inhabitants** thereof."

These words were meant to remind people of their freedom. Throughout American history, they have **inspired** those who wanted more rights. The writing on the Liberty Bell came to stand for many kinds of freedom for different groups of Americans.

The Liberty Bell is made of bronze. It weighs 2,080 pounds (943 kilograms). The bell's wooden mount is made of American elm.

# Where the Bell Began

In 1751, it had been 50 years since the founder of Pennsylvania, William Penn, created a **charter** that gave **colonists** many freedoms. The assembly, or lawmakers, wanted a bell to honor the charter.

A bell could also be used for other reasons. Pennsylvania lawmakers needed something to call their members to the state house for meetings. A bell was also a way to gather colonists to hear news.

So, a bell was ordered from England. Words on the bell tell who ordered it and for what place: "By Order of the Assembly of the Province of Pensylvania for the State House in Philad."

*William Penn*

In the days when the Liberty Bell was made, people spelled words in different ways. Pennsylvania is spelled "Pensylvania" on the bell. "Philad" is short for Philadelphia.

# The First Crack

The new bell, called the State House Bell, cracked the very first time it was rung! This is not the crack we see today, though. That bell was melted down in Philadelphia and the metal was used to make a new one. But this time, the bell did not sound right. The second bell was melted down and made yet again.

The lawmakers did not like the sound of the third bell, either. They ordered a brand new one from England. When the fourth bell arrived from overseas, lawmakers did not think it sounded any better. But the assembly decided to keep it. The State House Bell was housed in the Pennsylvania State House **steeple**. It was used to call the assembly of lawmakers together.

Metal workers John Pass and John Stow remade the bell both times. Their last names are recorded on the current bell.

## Ringing Throughout History

The State House Bell was rung at many important events during the time when the nation was forming. It played an important part in the birth of the United States. Many people think it was rung to call the assembly to meetings about British taxes on the colonies in the 1760s. These taxes were one reason the colonists later fought for independence. It may have also been rung to announce the battles at Lexington and Concord in 1775, the first of the American Revolution.

The bell was taken out of the steeple during the American Revolution. The colonists were worried that the British would melt it down and use the metal to make cannons. So, the State House Bell was moved to Allentown, Pennsylvania. It was hidden in the floor of a church to keep it safe. It was returned to the Pennsylvania State House in 1778.

No one knows for sure how the bell got its famous crack. Most believe it cracked in 1835 while ringing for a funeral of a Supreme Court justice.

## The Last Ring

In 1846, the city of Philadelphia wanted the bell to ring for George Washington's birthday. Metal workers drilled into the thin crack, making it wider and less likely to spread. But another crack began, starting at the abbreviation for Philadelphia and running up through the word "Liberty." The bell was never rung again.

A story in 1847 called "Ring, Grandfather, Ring" made the bell even more famous—for something that never happened! The story claimed that the bell was rung on July 4, 1776, to mark the signing of the Declaration of Independence. But that's not true. Instead, it was probably rung on July 8, 1776, to call people to hear the Declaration of Independence for the first time. But now, some historians think this is untrue too.

The Liberty Bell was rung for the last time to honor George Washington's birthday in 1846.

# Becoming the "Liberty Bell"

Abolitionists first called the bell the "Liberty Bell" in 1835. These people wanted to abolish, or do away with, slavery. The bell was a symbol for their movement. For them, the words on it meant that all people who lived in the United States should have their liberty.

After slavery ended following the American Civil War (1861–1865), the Liberty Bell was taken across the country for Americans to see. It was presented as a symbol of American freedom and a country united once again.

*The Liberty Bell does not ring anymore. Sometimes it is tapped, though.*

# Women's Rights Movement

The Women's Rights Movement of the early 1900s fought for women to have the same rights as men. The word *liberty* means "freedom," but also "a right." Groups of women used the Liberty Bell as a symbol for their fight for the right to vote.

A copy of the bell was made in 1915. It was known as the Justice Bell, or the Women's Liberty Bell. The **clapper** was chained to the bell's side, so that it could not ring until women were given the right to vote. Groups of women traveled across Pennsylvania with the bell to raise awareness for their movement.

In 1920, they finally received that right. The 19th amendment to the U.S. Constitution granted women the right to vote. The bell was rung in celebration.

Groups hoping to win certain rights still use the Liberty Bell as a symbol for their fight, just as the Women's Rights Movement did.

# Civil Rights of the 1960s

In the 1960s, many Black Americans were fighting for **civil rights**. Black people wanted their rights to be protected by the government, just like those of white people were.

In 1965, a group of 25 civil rights **advocates** staged a sit-in at the Liberty Bell at the state house, now called Independence Hall. A sit-in is a peaceful way to **protest** something that you disagree with. People sat in place to show they wanted fair treatment.

The protesting people sat around the famous symbol of American freedom. They hoped others would realize that the freedoms the bell symbolized were not enjoyed by all U.S. citizens. Later, laws were passed to provide civil rights for Black Americans.

The Liberty Bell is tapped gently each year on Martin Luther King Day to honor the famous Civil Rights leader and the Civil Rights Movement.

# Visiting the Liberty Bell

In 1976, the Liberty Bell was moved for a celebration of the nation's founding. In 2003, it was placed in a new building called Liberty Bell Center, which is part of Independence National Historic Park. The bell is now surrounded by glass, and Independence Hall can be seen beyond it.

About two million people visit the Liberty Bell each year. They want to see the symbol that has inspired people in the past to fight for the rights that we all enjoy today. The Liberty Bell is an American symbol that will continue to call people to fight for freedom and equality.

Each Fourth of July, the Liberty Bell is tapped 13 times. This is in honor of the 13 colonies that fought for the freedom of the United States from Great Britain.

# Activity: Fighting for Rights

**The Liberty Bell in Philadelphia is a symbol of freedom. Find out more about the groups that were inspired by the Liberty Bell to fight for their own freedoms.**

1. Draw an outline of a bell for each group of people inspired by the Liberty Bell.
2. On the mount of the bell, write the name of the group (for example, Women's Rights Movement).
3. Do research at the library or online to find out when and how each group achieved their goals.
4. Write what you learn in the body of the bell. (For example, the Voting Rights Act of 1965 outlawed practices that stopped Black Americans from voting.) There may be more than one answer in each bell.

# Glossary

**advocates** People who support an idea.

**charter** A piece of writing by a government that gives rights to a group.

**civil rights** The rights that should protect every person's freedom.

**clapper** The metal tongue of a bell that makes noise by banging on the side.

**colonist** A person who lives in a new country.

**inhabitant** A person who lives in a certain place.

**inspire** To make someone want to do something.

**proclaim** To announce loudly.

**protest** To show or express strong disagreement with something.

**steeple** A tall, pointed tower.

**symbol** An object that stands for something else.

# Index



# Learn More

**Liberty Bell**
*https://kids.britannica.com/students/article/Liberty-Bell/438419*
Learn about the history of the Liberty Bell at Britannica Kids.

**The Liberty Bell**
*https://www.nps.gov/inde/learn/historyculture/stories-liberty-bell.htm*
Read more about the Liberty Bell and find out where you can visit it.

**Publisher's note to educators and parents:** Our editors have carefully reviewed these websites to ensure that they are suitable for students. Many websites change frequently, however, and we cannot guarantee that a site's future contents will continue to meet our high standards of quality and educational value. Be advised that students should be closely supervised whenever they access the Internet.